CITIES OF THE
WORLD

VIENNA

BY R. CONRAD STEIN

CHILDREN'S PRESS®
A Division of Grolier Publishing
New York London Hong Kong Sydney
Danbury, Connecticut

CONSULTANTS

Peter Hayes, Ph.D.
Alfred W. Chase Professor
Department of History
Northwestern University

Linda Cornwell
Learning Resource Consultant
Indiana Department of Education

Project Editor: Downing Publishing Services
Design Director: Karen Kohn & Associates, Ltd.
Photo Researcher: Jan Izzo
Pronunciations: Courtesy of Tony Breed, M.A., Linguistics, University of Chicago, with assistance from Maria Wendel, German Instructor

---

NOTES ON GERMAN PRONUNCIATION

The words in this book are pronounced basically the way the pronunciation guides look. There are a few notes, however: *ah* is like *a* in father; *a* is as in can; *ar* is as in far; *ai* and *ay* are like *ai* in rain; *aw* is as in draw; *oh*, *oa*, and *oe* are like *o* in rope; *ow* and *aow* are always as *ow* in cow, never as in tow; *u* and *uh* are very short and quick, like *a* in about; *igh* is as in light. In German, there is no soft *g* as in gentle; it is always hard, as in give. The sound *h̲* does not occur in English. It is like the *h* in hat but stronger and harsher. If you try to say *k* as in kite but relax and slur the sound, it will sound like *h̲*. *Pf* sounds exactly as it is spelled, like *pf* in cupful.

Visit Children's Press on the Internet at: http://publishing.grolier.com

---

Library of Congress Cataloging-in-Publication Data

Stein, R. Conrad.
  Vienna / by R. Conrad Stein.
    p. cm. — (Cities of the world)
  Includes bibliographical references and index.
  Summary: Describes the history, culture, daily life, food, people, sports, and points of interest in the capital and largest city in Austria.
  ISBN 0-516-20789-X
  1. Vienna (Austria)—Juvenile literature.   [1. Vienna (Austria)]
I. Title.   II. Series: Cities of the world (New York, N.Y.)
D8847.S78   1998   98-22248
943.6'13—dc21   CIP
                                                         AC

1 2 3 4 5 6 7 8 9 10 R 07 06 05 04 03 02 01 00 99 98

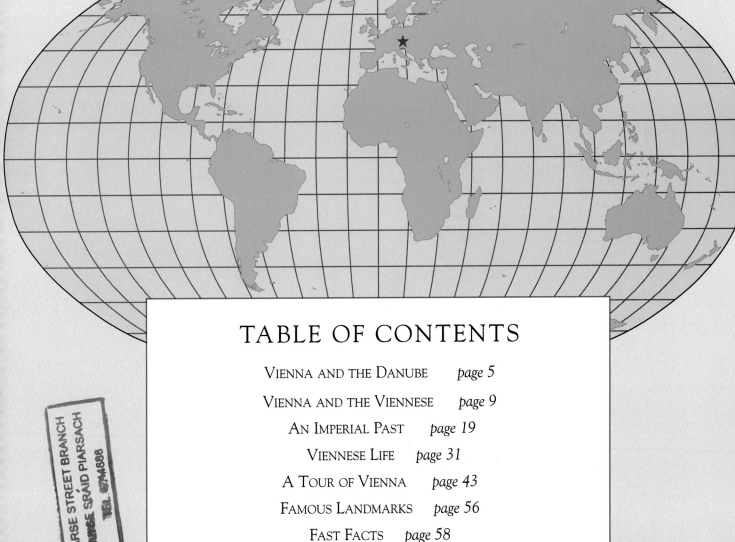

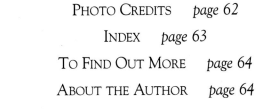

TABLE OF CONTENTS

More than one hundred years ago, Johann Strauss Jr. wrote a waltz called "On the Beautiful Blue Danube." The music praised Vienna, the great European city on the Danube River. It was a wonderful piece of music, but it posed a couple of problems. First, the stream that flows through old Vienna is the Danube Canal, not the actual river. Second, its color is muddy grey or green. Never are the Danube's waters blue. Did Strauss lie to us? If so, the city of Vienna forgives him. Strauss is a musician, and musicians are heroes in old Vienna.

Vienna was once the capital of the Austrian Empire, a vast territory that stretched from Switzerland to Russia. It was a storybook kingdom of princes and princesses. In the old days, the royal families built palaces in the capital. They collected fabulous paintings and statues. They danced at lavish balls held in their palaces. Today, the empire and the emperors are a distant dream. Vienna is now the capital only of the relatively small nation of Austria. Still, memories of its glory days linger in the city's art, architecture, food, and especially in its music. For this reason, tourists and students flock to Vienna, a city of the ages.

Vienna (VEE-ENN-UH)
Danube (DAN-YOOB)

A Viennese folk-
art box (left)
and a Viennese
Christmas tree
ornament (right)

This painting of a Vienna State Ball captures the lavish
lifestyle of wealthy nineteenth-century Viennese royalty.

This [Vienna] is one of the most perplexing cities that I was ever in. . . . It has immense palaces, superb galleries of paintings, theaters. . . . In short everything bears the stamp of luxury; for here is assembled all the wealth, fashion, and nobility of the Austrian Empire.

—American visitor
Washington Irving, writing
to his sister in
November 1822

A RIDE ON THE RING

Modern Vienna has excellent public transportation. Passengers ride streetcars, buses, a subway, and an elevated train system. Tourists are advised to take the streetcars marked numbers 1 and 2. Those streetcars roll over the Ringstrasse (Ring Street). It is a tree-lined boulevard that forms a half ring around Vienna's historic heart. Long ago, the old city walls stood on what is now Ring Street. Today, the street offers a panorama of centuries-old buildings. Each of the buildings has a story to tell.

From the streetcar window, a passenger looks out at the State Opera House. It is an extravagant structure built in 1869. Its outside walls are covered with gingerbread designs. But shortly after it was built,

the Austrian emperor said he was not pleased with the Opera House's looks. Upon hearing the remark, one of the architects shot himself to death and the other died of grief.

Emperor Franz Josef was horrified that his criticism caused the architects such devastating pain. Thereafter, when inspecting a new Vienna building, he always said, "It is very nice. It pleases me very much."

A streetcar rider on the Ringstrasse will also see the Hofburg Palace. It is a complex of buildings that were built slowly, ever so slowly. In fact, the Hofburg's building process went on for 700 years. Construction on Hofburg's Neue Burg (New Wing) began in 1881. And the New Wing is the newest part of the building complex. The Belvedere Palace is a quick walk from the Ringstrasse. It was once the summer palace of a courageous soldier named Prince Eugene of Savoy. The prince let his pet lions roam free in the palace gardens.

It takes about twenty-five minutes for the streetcar to complete a cycle on the U-shaped Ringstrasse. During the course of the trip, scores of passengers leave and enter. Amazingly, no one pays for tickets or gives money to the driver. Is the streetcar ride free? No. People buy a weekly or monthly pass that allows them unlimited trips on the public transit system. Inspectors sometimes ride the system and ask to see the passes. Rarely does a passenger encounter one of these inspectors. In truth, paying for rides is on the honor system. Few people cheat. Vienna is a clean and orderly city, and the Viennese strive to keep it that way.

Opposite page: The Opera House

Ringstrasse (RING-SHTRAH-SUH)
Hofburg (HOAF-BOORK)
Neue Burg (NOY-UH BOORK)
Belvedere (BELL-VEH-DARE)
fiaker (FEE-AH-CARE)

The Horse Cab

Another way to get around the city is in a *fiaker*, a horse-drawn carriage. There are dozens of such carriages in Vienna. The front of St. Stefan's Cathedral is a popular gathering place for the horse cabs. A trip by carriage around the Ringstrasse is an expensive ride, usually taken by tourists. But for a treat, even native Viennese enjoy an occasional buggy ride.

11

A LOOK AT THE VIENNESE

A view of the main altar in St. Stefan's Cathedral

The towering St. Stefan's Cathedral (Stephansdom) is Vienna's most prominent landmark. It is also one of its oldest structures. Parts of St. Stefan's date back to the 1200s. The Viennese call the building "Old Steffl." Car traffic is prohibited on most of the streets near St. Stefan's. The area is a pedestrian mall crammed with shops, restaurants, and theaters. Always crowded, the St. Stefan's neighborhood is a perfect place to observe the Viennese.

There is no typical Viennese look. The vast majority of Viennese speak German, and they observe many German customs. But the city has always been a crossroads where various ethnic groups have met and settled down. Just a quick walk around St. Stefan's reveals dark-haired Mediterranean people as well as blond northern European types. Africans and Asians are also present in large numbers.

Most Viennese are Catholic. Church celebrations rule much of city life. Lent is a solemn time when the Viennese give up their favorite foods to honor the suffering of Jesus Christ. *Fasching* is the joyous party season held before Lent. During Fasching, everyone is permitted to go a little crazy at the city's many dances and parties. The Viennese also dress up their children for special church occasions such as a child's first Holy Communion.

A Viennese fiaker coachman

Steffl (STEFF-UHL)
Fasching (FAH-SHING)

12

St. Stefan's, a Survivor of Many Wars

Over the centuries, St. Stefan's Cathedral has been battered many times by battles raging in or near Vienna. A cannonball fired hundreds of years ago by a Turkish army is still embedded in one of the church's walls. The building's worst damage came after a World War II bombing raid. Bombs caused the church to burst into a roaring fire that collapsed the roof and the upper walls. After the war, laborers worked for more than ten years to rebuild this beloved cathedral.

Some observers claim the Viennese are showy in the way they dress. It is said that they enjoy parading about the streets while wearing very formal clothes. Certainly, many people browsing at the shops have spotless suits and dresses, all in the latest fashion. This tendency to dress up may date back to the time of the empire. Royal rank once held sway over every detail of city life. Even non-nobles wanted to imitate the nobility. Therefore, today's men and women spend a little extra money to buy the very finest clothes.

Along St. Stefan's Plaza are hordes of street entertainers. The street musicians and actors dress any way they please. A strikingly beautiful young lady imitates a statue. She is painted white, wears a Roman toga, and stands as if frozen to the sidewalk. Street artists paint people's portraits for a small fee. A

Right: A patch showing the Vienna (Wien) coat of arms
Below: This street performer in St. Stefan's Plaza is dressed as a clown.

Mozart (MOATS-AHRT)
Naschmarkt (NAHSH-MARKTK)

Shoppers on Kartnerstrasse (above left) dress more formally than those who frequent the Nashmarkt (above).

string quartet plays the music of Mozart. Puppeteers draw giggling crowds of kids as well as interested adults. One wooden puppet-on-a-string is brilliantly designed to look like the American singing idol Elvis Presley. The puppeteer plays music from a portable cassette player while the Elvis figure dances with hip-swiveling moves to "You Ain't Nothin' but a Hound Dog."

For centuries, Vienna has accepted people from foreign lands—Czechs, Hungarians, Poles,

Romanians. Workers from the former Soviet Union are the newest immigrants. At a flea market called the Mexico Plaza, the former Soviets buy goods and exchange gossip about their home countries. Vendors bark out prices and haggle in their native languages. The Mexico Plaza is a virtual babble of tongues.

The city's most popular market is the Naschmarkt. For decades, the Naschmarkt consisted of open-air food stands where farmers brought their produce. The

stands are still there. Apples sold at the Naschmarkt are so good the Viennese call them "paradise apples." The women who run the stands are known to tease customers and tell off-color jokes. On Saturdays, special market stalls are set up and vendors offer secondhand items for sale. The

cat-calling food sellers and the hawkers of goods make the Naschmarkt a wonderful place to enjoy the color of Vienna.

THE PRATER

The Prater is Vienna's beloved playground. It is a 3,200-acre (1,295-hectare) city park with an amusement arcade at one end and miles of grass and trees along the other. Like everything else in Vienna, the park grounds have deep historical roots. At one time, the land was a private hunting and riding area reserved for royalty. Then in 1766, Emperor Joseph II gave the Prater to the people of Vienna. They have enjoyed it as a park ever since.

The Prater's amusement park is busy day and night. It is dominated by the 212-foot (65-meter) Ferris wheel, a city landmark. The great wheel was put up in 1897. It is the only survivor of similar devices that once stood in Paris, London, and Chicago. Passengers ride in small cabins and enjoy a breathtaking view of the city. Other attractions include roller coasters and merry-go-rounds. During the day, small children come to the amusement park with their parents. At night, the entertainment gets a little more gaudy as taverns open and shows featuring dancing girls begin.

The Ferris wheel at the Prater

Prater (PRAH-TARE)
Burggarten (BOORK-GAHR-TEN)
Volksgarten (FOLKS-GAHR-TEN))

The Volksgarten rose gardens are famous the world over.

The Prater parklands are a favorite get-away spot for families. Cars are not allowed in the park. The grounds are so vast that families can have a picnic surrounded by trees and grass with not one city building in sight. Joggers and bicyclists race along park lanes.

On weekend afternoons, a dozen soccer games take place.

Of course, the Prater is not Vienna's only city park. Vienna boasts more than 800 parks spread throughout its metropolitan area. Two beloved inner-city parks are the Burggarten and the Volksgarten. The Volksgarten is world-famous for its rose gardens.

Still, the Prater holds a special place in the hearts of the Viennese. Young people get married in the park. Large families hold reunions there and attract hundreds of distant relatives. The Prater is a historic park. And the Viennese have a keen awareness of their city's history.

Celtic people settled on the site of Vienna more than 2,000 years ago. The Romans established a frontier post there in 15 B.C. The village was then called Vindobona. Its strategic location on the Danube River made it important. The Danube was Europe's prime highway. So even in ancient times, Vienna was a crossroads and a meeting place for a wide variety of people.

Vindobona (VEEN-DOE-BOHN-UH)

THE ROYAL HAPSBURGS

The key date in Vienna's history is the year 1278. That year, Count Rudolf Hapsburg (often spelled Habsburg), the king of Germany, took possession of Vienna and all the surrounding land.

The count made Vienna headquarters for the powerful Hapsburg family. The Hapsburgs ruled the city for the next 640 years.

Because of its commanding location on the Danube, Vienna was coveted by invading armies. In 1529 and again in 1683, Turkish forces attacked Vienna. The Turks could not pierce the city's thick walls. The warfare, while horrible, added to the city's lore. At one point, the

Turks tried to assault Vienna by tunneling under the walls. Bakers, working at night, heard the tunneling and alerted the army. Ever since then, bakers have been heroes in Vienna. According to

In the year 1273, Count Rudolf I, a member of the Hapsburg family, was elected Holy Roman Emperor.

Above: Turks attacking Vienna in 1529

legend, the Turks left several sacks of coffee beans behind when they retreated. This was the first coffee the Viennese had ever seen, and it began a city tradition. The modern city has more than 2,000 coffeehouses.

Century by century, the Hapsburgs expanded their empire. Over the years, the empire was called various names: the Archduchy of Austria, the Austrian Empire, and Austria-Hungary. Always Vienna was its capital and always the Hapsburgs were in power. Often the Hapsburgs did not wage war to enlarge their territory. Instead, they married their daughters and sons to European royal families and inherited land in the process. Some marriages had tragic results. In 1770, the Hapsburg daughter Marie Antoinette married Louis XVI, who became king of France. She was beheaded during the French Revolution by people who hated the monarchy.

Left: Louis XVI and Marie Antoinette with their son, the dauphin (crown prince)

Hapsburg (HOPS-boork)

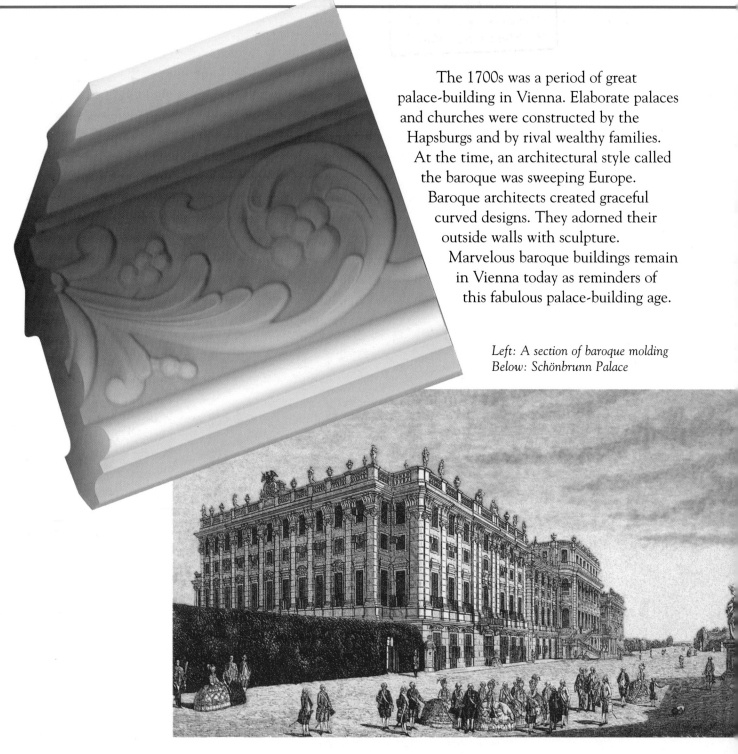

The 1700s was a period of great palace-building in Vienna. Elaborate palaces and churches were constructed by the Hapsburgs and by rival wealthy families. At the time, an architectural style called the baroque was sweeping Europe. Baroque architects created graceful curved designs. They adorned their outside walls with sculpture. Marvelous baroque buildings remain in Vienna today as reminders of this fabulous palace-building age.

Left: A section of baroque molding
Below: Schönbrunn Palace

One of the greatest of the Hapsburg builders was Maria Theresa, who ascended to the throne in 1740. She is called the mother of both Vienna and Austria. A mother she certainly was. Maria Theresa had sixteen children. She wanted nothing but the best for her enormous family, so Maria Theresa built the great Schönbrunn Palace just outside the city walls. When completed, the palace had 1,200 rooms. Each child had five rooms and was attended by five servants.

Empress Maria Theresa (left) built the 1,200-room Schönbrunn Palace.

Schönbrunn
(SHOOHN-BROON)

IMPERIAL LIFE

What was life like for the noble families whose monuments still grace Vienna? Certainly, they suffered the tragedies of sickness and death equally with the peasants. The rich, however, were able to surround their families with paintings, sculpture, fine food, and—most important—music. Wealthy Viennese built concert halls in their palaces. They commissioned court composers to work for their families. The court composers gave lessons to children, and they wrote music designed to enhance the family's prestige. In the eighteenth and nineteenth centuries, musical legends worked as court composers in Vienna: Glück, Haydn, Mozart, Beethoven, Brahms, and many more.

This legion of composers began Vienna's Golden Age of Music. For almost two centuries, Vienna was the capital of musical life in the Western world. Modern Viennese think of the composers as heroes and study their life stories.

Beethoven was a short-tempered man who roamed the woods outside town while writing magnificent musical scores in his head. Profoundly deaf much of his adult life, he still composed masterpieces. His Ninth Symphony and his opera *Fidelio*, both of which were written in Vienna, are triumphant works. They are enjoyed by millions of people today.

The saddest story of all the composers is that of Wolfgang Amadeus Mozart. A musical prodigy, he wrote symphonies before he was fourteen. Born in Salzburg, Austria, Mozart did his greatest work while living in Vienna. In

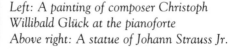

Left: A painting of composer Christoph Willibald Glück at the pianoforte
Above right: A statue of Johann Strauss Jr.

Glück (GLEWK)
Haydn (HIDE-un)
Beethoven (BAY-toe-venn)
Brahms (BRAHMZ)
Fidelio (FEE-DAY-lee-oh)
Salzburg (SAHLTS-boork)

A portrait of Ludwig von Beethoven holding a score

A pillbox with a portrait of Mozart

W. A. MOZART

1782, he was married at St. Stefan's Cathedral. Nine years later, at the age of thirty-four, Mozart died. His funeral mass was held at St. Stefan's. The Viennese never truly appreciated Mozart's gifts. Deeply in debt, he was buried in an unmarked grave. Now Mozart is one of Vienna's greatest heroes. It is safe to say that not an evening goes by without a Mozart opera, symphony, or chamber music piece being performed somewhere in the city on the Danube.

In 1848, Franz Josef, a Hapsburg, ascended to power. He ruled Vienna and Austria for the next 68 years. He also ruled the neighboring Kingdom of Hungary. In his time, Vienna's old city walls were torn down to create the Ringstrasse, the beautiful boulevard that defines Vienna today. The city grew to a population of 600,000. The Austrian Empire and the Kingdom of Hungary became a dual monarchy in 1867, and Vienna glittered as the capital of Austria-Hungary.

Music continued to fill the air during the time of Franz Josef. Johann Strauss Jr. wrote his gorgeous waltzes. Ballroom dancing was the rage of Vienna high society. The military was a glamorous profession under Franz Josef. Balls featured straight-backed army officers wearing colorful uniforms. The officers waltzed with pretty women dressed in flowing gowns. Dancing was so socially important that schools to teach young people proper ballroom etiquette flourished in the capital. Young men were instructed in the correct way to present their card when asking a young woman for a dance. Young

Above right: Emperor Franz Josef

Right: During the time of Franz Josef, ballroom dancing was the rage of Viennese high society.

women learned to flutter their fans with appropriate grace.

The reign of Franz Josef was the last chapter in the storybook empire. In 1914, a fanatical student shot and killed Archduke Franz Ferdinand, the Hapsburg heir to the Austro-Hungarian throne. Leaders in Vienna believed the assassination was part of a plot to overthrow Austria-Hungary. The assassination led to World War I.

The 1914 asssassination of Archduke Franz Ferdinand, heir to the Austro-Hungarian throne (shown here with his wife, Countess Cholek), led to World War I.

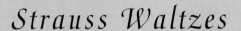

Walzer
(VAHLT-SARE)
walzen
(VAHLT-SENN)

Strauss Waltzes

In the early 1800s, Vienna-born Johann Strauss Sr. composed dance tunes that were called *Walzers*. The term comes from the German word *walzen*, meaning to turn around. Strauss waltzes were a hit with the city's music lovers. Though he was successful as a composer and bandmaster, Johann Strauss Sr. hoped his son would choose some profession other than music. Pretending to obey his father's wishes, the son, Johann Strauss Jr., worked as a clerk in a Vienna bank. But unbeknownst to the father, the younger Strauss conducted his own waltz band at night. He also wrote music, including "Tales of the Vienna Woods" and "Vienna Blood." These works are among the most famous waltzes of all time.

VIENNA IN THE TWENTIETH CENTURY

World War I ended in 1918, a crushing defeat for Germany and its principal ally, Austria-Hungary. After the war, the Austro-Hungarian Empire was dismantled and the German-speaking territory around Vienna became the Republic of Austria. A republic is a nation without a king or queen. Never again would royalty rule Vienna or Austria.

Even before World War I, the seeds of a new European conflict were planted in Vienna. In 1907, an eighteen-year-old art student named Adolf Hitler moved to the city. He was denied admission to the Vienna Academy of Fine Arts because teachers questioned his

The Vienna State Opera House was badly damaged by a bombing raid during World War II.

talent as a painter. Hitler tried to sell his paintings to art dealers but found few customers. He stayed in Vienna doing odd jobs such as carrying suitcases at the railroad station. Vienna was home to Jews, Slavs, and other ethnic groups. The would-be artist grew bitter watching these non-Germans prosper.

Hitler returned to Vienna in triumph in 1938. He was now the head of the German state. As chancellor of Germany, the Austrian-born Hitler succeeded in uniting Austria with Germany. Such a union had long been a dream for many German-speaking people. Tens of thousands of Viennese lined the streets to cheer Hitler as his car rolled by. However, the union with Germany pulled Austria into World War II. During the war, Vienna was controlled by the German army. Jews and political rebels were rounded up and taken to concentration camps.

As the war continued, Vienna suffered countless air raids. The bombings killed 12,000 people. Some 20 percent of the city's housing was destroyed. Great landmarks such as St. Stefan's and the giant Ferris wheel at the Prater were damaged. Almost 25 percent of the people were made homeless. In 1945, Soviet troops took possession of a battered Vienna whose citizens were near starvation.

For ten years, Vienna and Austria were occupied by soldiers from the Soviet Union, the United States, France, and Great Britain. The occupation was a bitter period, but it was also a time of rebuilding. Bomb-damaged houses and apartment buildings were repaired. Always mindful of their golden past, the Viennese took great care to reconstruct palaces and churches to look exactly as they had before the war. In

1955, the occupation ended. Vienna was a free and independent city once more.

Vienna prospered in the 1970s and 1980s. The subway system expanded and new hotels were built. The huge United Nations Center, a complex of office buildings, was finished in 1979. The improvements thrust old Vienna into the modern world. But it remained a city proud of its imperial past.

A British officer patrols the street in front of a bomb-damaged Vienna hotel after a 1948 bomb explosion.

The Viennese love the story of Johann Strauss Jr., who is called the "Waltz King." Yes, the son defied his father by secretly becoming a musician. But the younger Strauss was virtually exploding with musical talent. He could not expect to enjoy life as a bank clerk. And the enjoyment of life is paramount in Viennese thinking. The Viennese celebrate life in their food, parties, sports, music, and art. Visitors are easily drawn into the city's zest for living. Vienna is a place that strives to entertain both residents and guests.

FABULOUS FOOD

A *Sachertorte* is a sinfully rich chocolate cake made with a secret recipe. This very special cake was invented about 150 years ago by a chef working in Vienna's Sacher Hotel. For generations, it was sold only at the hotel's cafe. The chocolate delight enjoyed worldwide fame as Vienna's tastiest pastry. Then in the 1960s, a rival café copied the recipe and sold its own brand of Sachertorte. Enraged, the Sacher Hotel owner sued in court. The Sacher Hotel won the case. An indignant judge said the rivals had no right to make off with a time-honored recipe. The conflict illustrates that in Vienna—and perhaps only in Vienna—will restaurants sue each other over the right to sell a piece of cake.

To the Viennese, eating is a celebration of life, not just a necessity of life. In their homes they serve delicious meals, delicately prepared. When dining out, they demand food that is better than the meals they make at home. As a result, the city has a wonderful array of restaurants, cafes, and coffeehouses.

Sachertorte (below) is only one of the many rich pastries for which Vienna is famous.

Sachertorte (SAH-HARE-TORE-TUH)
Sacher (SAH-HARE)
Heuriger (HOY-REEG-AIR)
goulash (GOO-LAHSH)
weiner schnitzel (VEE-NARE SHNIT-SELL)

An antique café sign in Vienna

The Heuriger

The woods and fields outside Vienna have long been wine-making country. Each year when the new wine is made, the wine shops (called *Heuriger*) practice an old tradition. The establishments hang a bunch of pine branches over their entrances to announce that the new wine is ready to be served. Nondrinkers may enter a Heuriger and still enjoy themselves because the shops also offer grand buffets of hardy country-made stews.

Favorite restaurant dishes include *goulash* (a veal stew) and *weiner schnitzel* (a breaded veal cutlet). Venison (deer meat) is also on many menus. The preference for venison is another aspect of Vienna life that is rooted in the past. At one time, only kings and princes were allowed to hunt deer. The Viennese middle class always tried to imitate the nobility. Today, venison dishes served at restaurants let people imagine they are eating like kings.

Restaurants try to impress their customers with attractive settings as well as fine meals. In expensive restaurants, tablecloths are starchy white and are topped with a vase of flowers. Waiters and waitresses dress in costumes designed to look like eighteenth-century Austrian farmers. In this history-minded city, the past is glorified whenever possible. A restaurant on Fleischmarkt (meat market) Street claims to have been a public eating establishment since the 1500s. Over the years, the owners have encouraged famous guests to write their names on the walls. Today, waiters proudly point out the fading signatures of such luminaries as Beethoven, Mozart, the Strausses (father and son), and American writer Mark Twain.

Vienna is both a modern and an international city. Its restaurants reflect the diverse population. Turkish, Yugoslav, and Albanian cafés stand beside places that offer Chinese or Thai food. Fast-food restaurants such as McDonald's are popular with the young people. Older Viennese consider the meal-a-minute establishments to be an insult to eating.

No one denies the fast-food places are the most inexpensive way to eat in this very expensive city. A "Big Mac" and a soft drink in a Vienna McDonald's costs between five and six dollars, a high price by North American standards. But even an inexpensive lunch in a traditional restaurant costs three times the price of a McDonald's meal. At the better restaurants, one is charged even for bread. A server might present a customer with a basket of ten bread rolls. If seven rolls remain in the basket, the customer must pay for eating three.

Most Viennese have their main meal at noon.

Opposite page, bottom left: A Vienna coffeehouse
Left: An outdoor restaurant in Vienna
Above: A waiter at a Vienna café
Right: A gift package of Vienna's famous coffee

At night, they crowd into coffeehouses for snacks. Coffeehouses are small, cozy places that sell mainly coffee and desserts. Many Viennese use a favorite coffeehouse as a home-away-from-home. Regular customers will sit at a *Stammtisch*, their own reserved table. Some customers even receive mail at their coffeehouses. Prices are high, but people can sit and chat over cups of coffee for as long as they wish. Some play cards or chess. Waiters bring newspapers to customers sitting alone. Many coffeehouses employ a small string orchestra to play the works of Mozart or Strauss while the evening crowds relax.

MUSIC AND DANCE —STILL A VIENNA PASSION

Years ago, greatness fed upon greatness to make Vienna the musical capital of Europe. In the 1860s, composer Johannes Brahms called Vienna the "musician's holy city." In old Vienna, musicians tutored one another, counseled one another, and attended one

Left: Johannes Brahms
Below: The State Opera House

Street musicians on Kartnerstrasse

another's concerts. Brahms moved from Hamburg, Germany, to Vienna so he could "drink the wine Beethoven drank."

Perhaps a budding genius is writing great music in a Vienna flat today. Perhaps future generations will applaud his or her symphonies. Perhaps. But most music lovers come to the modern city to listen, not to create. Vienna is a musical shrine, a place where one can thrill to the music of the masters in their own special city. Yes, American-style rock music is played in Vienna. But even many of the city's young people favor the classics over the pounding beats of rock.

Two major opera houses stand in Vienna. The *Staatsoper* (State's Opera) is one of the world's greatest performing centers. Built in 1869, it was almost leveled during World War II. It was reconstructed over a ten-year period and now serves a full audience nearly every night. Tickets are less expensive and easier to obtain at the *Volksoper* (People's Opera), but the performances there are just as rewarding. The Viennese regularly bring their children to the opera. Amazingly, children as young as nine or ten sit in rapt attention as they watch the grand operas of Mozart and Wagner.

Four full symphony orchestras make Vienna their home. The Vienna Philharmonic is hailed as one of the world's finest orchestras. Scores of chamber-music groups, called ensembles, perform in the city. Most chamber-music ensembles have two to six members. Near St. Stefan's Cathedral, a chamber ensemble plays Mozart pieces in a tiny room where Mozart once lived and worked. The musicians wear clothes and white wigs typical of the Mozart era.

Waltzes and the excitement of ballroom dancing still thrive in Vienna.

Costumed musicians at a Viennese Mozart festival

About 300 balls are held during *Fasching*, the holiday season celebrated just before Lent. Doctors hold a ball, as do lawyers and firemen. The most famous ball takes place in the State Opera House. It is a costume ball. Everyone dresses like elegant ladies and gentlemen of imperial times. Many restaurants offer dinner concerts where non-dancers enjoy the

music of Strauss while they eat.

The Vienna Boys' Choir is a world-famous institution. It was founded as a chapel choir in 1498. Today, it consists of 88 boys, divided into four groups. Ranging in age from about eleven through thirteen, the boys are specially selected for their sweet voices. They live in dormitories at Vienna's plush

Augarten Palace. There they receive an academic as well as a musical education. And they travel. The Vienna Boys' Choir packs concert halls throughout the world. Despite their globe-trotting, the boys remain a Vienna church group. Parishioners must get tickets months in advance if they wish to hear the boys sing at Sunday Mass in the Imperial Chapel of the Hofburg Palace.

The Philharmonic Ball (left) is one of many balls held during Fasching.

The Vienna Boys' Choir

SPORTS AND FUN

More than 300 miles (483 kilometers) of official bicycle paths weave through Vienna. Bicycling is not just a sport. Many cyclists ride their bikes to school and to work every day. Boating on the Danube is a fun activity. During the summer, a variety of craft—paddleboats, kayaks, and rowboats—take to the waters. At one time, the Danube waters looked and smelled like a sewer. Now, the river has been cleaned up to the point where it is swimmable in some sections.

In the winter, outdoor ice skating is popular with the Viennese. Many families go skating after mass on Sundays. Like so much else in the Austrian capital, skating is accompanied by music. Speakers resonate with Strauss or the other waltz masters as the skaters twirl on the ice. A traditional skating section near the Heurmarkt is roped off in rings. The outer skating ring is reserved for expert dancers, while the inner ring holds the struggling amateurs.

Boys on a Vienna street pose on their bicycles.

Soccer is the favorite spectator sport for the Viennese. Major matches are played at the Vienna Stadium in Prater Park. Also in the Prater is a popular horse-racing track. A highlight for horse-racing fans is the Derby that takes place on the third Sunday in June. During Derby Day, high-society people come to be seen as well as to enjoy the excitement of the races. It is customary for ladies and gentlemen to wear their finest clothes to Vienna's Derby. Well-to-do people consider Derby Day to be about as elegant as a fancy costume ball.

Many Viennese and visitors watch a different horse spectacle—the shows put on by the famous Spanish Riding School. Regular eighty-minute shows are held at the Hofburg Palace. The tradition of the riding school dates back to the days of the Austrian cavalry. The horses came originally from Spain. According to a king's order, issued long ago, the horses must be white. Two teams of horses and riders march in interweaving patterns, always accompanied by music. People watching these precision riding exhibitions compare them with a ballet dance.

Precision horseback riding at the Spanish Riding School

A Spanish Riding School plaque

Heumarkt (HOY-MARKT)

Vienna is one of Europe's leading tourist cities. Every year, millions of foreigners come to see the sights, sample the food, and hear the music. There is so much to see and do that tourists need to organize their visits. A good approach is to break a tour into three primary areas: the inner city, the Ringstrasse, and the outlying sights.

VIENNA'S HISTORIC HEART

Vienna's inner city stretches from the Danube Canal out to the horseshoe-shaped Ringstrasse. In this region, Vienna began as a small Celtic settlement some 2,000 years ago. The ancient neighborhood contains many historical monuments. It is also the modern city's most fashionable shopping and entertainment area.

Rising over the heart of the inner city is St. Stefan's Cathedral. More than 700 years old, the building is Vienna's special treasure. And it remains a functioning church. Guests are asked to be mindful of worshipers and not to treat the place as if it were a museum. St. Stefan's inner walls are covered with sculptures of religious figures. A striking feature is the stone pulpit, carved in about 1510. Visitors climb the steep 345 steps of an interior staircase to reach the church steeple. It is a tough, ten-minute climb even for a young person. But the view is worth the effort. On a clear day, all of Vienna can be seen from the top of this beloved church.

An interior view of St. Stefan's Cathedral

A pattern of shingles on the roof of St. Stefan's Cathedral

When exploring the streets near St. Stefan's, it is a good idea to bring a guidebook and let the buildings tell you stories. A placard marks a house called the Pasqualatihaus, once Beethoven's residence. While he lived there, Beethoven wrote some of his greatest works, including his only opera, *Fidelio.*

Another house, known as Basiliskenhaus, has the carved figure of a frog on its outside wall. According to legend, in the year 1212 an incredibly ugly frog hopped into a well here and created a stench that fouled the whole city. A heroic young boy climbed into the well armed only with a mirror. The boy let the frog see itself in the mirror. The frog, terrified by its own ugliness, turned instantly to stone.

A Viennese folk-art bell

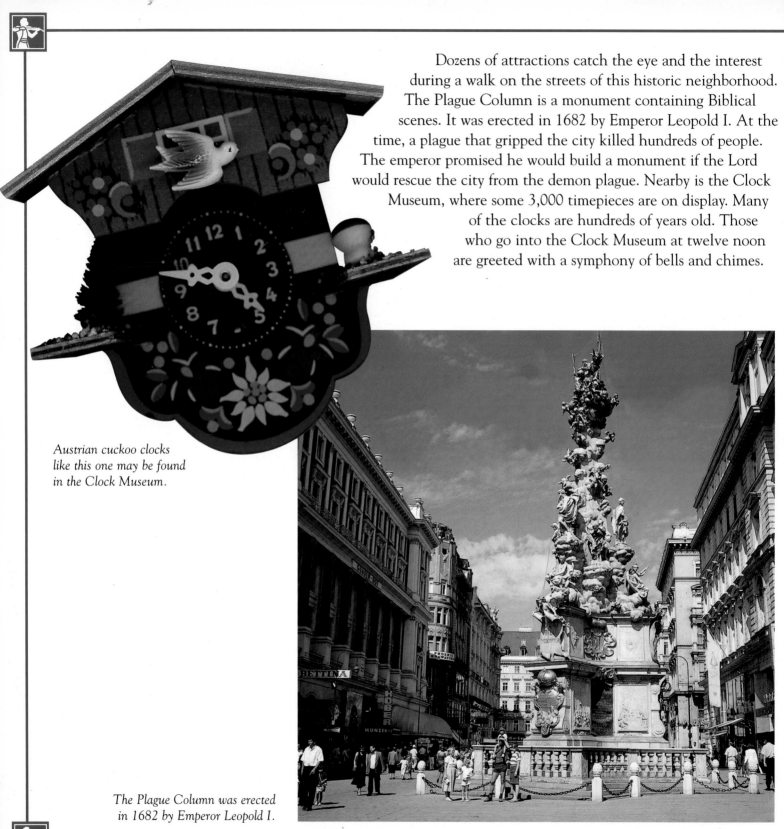

Dozens of attractions catch the eye and the interest during a walk on the streets of this historic neighborhood. The Plague Column is a monument containing Biblical scenes. It was erected in 1682 by Emperor Leopold I. At the time, a plague that gripped the city killed hundreds of people. The emperor promised he would build a monument if the Lord would rescue the city from the demon plague. Nearby is the Clock Museum, where some 3,000 timepieces are on display. Many of the clocks are hundreds of years old. Those who go into the Clock Museum at twelve noon are greeted with a symphony of bells and chimes.

Austrian cuckoo clocks like this one may be found in the Clock Museum.

The Plague Column was erected in 1682 by Emperor Leopold I.

Inner-city Vienna has many cafes and restaurants. One coffeehouse is the Café Vienna, famous for baking the biggest cakes in the city. The Café Central was once a hangout for artists, writers, and musicians. Struggling artists avoid the Café Central now because a cup of coffee there costs almost as much as a full meal somewhere else. But it costs nothing to sit in a park. A restful green island is the Stadtpark along the Ringstrasse. Rising above the park is an impressive statue of Johann Strauss Jr. The Viennese are generous in building statues for their musical geniuses. In various parts of the city are monuments to Beethoven, Brahms, Mozart, and Franz Schubert.

This statue of Johann Strauss Jr. stands in the Stadtpark.

Stadtpark (SHTOT-PARK)

RING STREET

German poet Goethe called architecture "frozen music." Few other places in the world display frozen music in the style of the Ringstrasse. Thick walls of the old city once stood here. It was fashionable for royalty to build palaces just outside those city walls. When the walls were removed in the 1850s, the palaces remained. Then Europe's best architects were called in to design churches and government buildings

The Burgtheater

City Hall (the Rathaus)

to complement the palaces. As a result, the Ringstrasse has a parade of extravagant buildings such as City Hall, the Parliament, and the Burgtheater. All these grand structures recall the glory of the Austrian Empire.

Palaces along the Ringstrasse route get the most attention from tourists. Until 1918, the Hofburg Palace was the home of the ruling Hapsburg family. The Hofburg is a series of buildings built over 700 years. Today, it is a museum complex where thousands visit daily. The Neue Burg section contains four museums, including the popular Collection of Musical Instruments and the Collection of Weapons. To the east is the Museum of Fine Arts, which houses one of the most stunning arrays of artwork in the world. Also within the palace are the Royal Apartments, home to the president of Austria.

Burgtheater (BOORK-TAY-AH-TARE)

The Hofburg Palace

Belvedere Palace was built in the early 1700s just outside the old city walls. The Belvedere (the name means "beautiful view") was the palace of Prince Eugene of Savoy, Austria's greatest military commander. Belvedere is made up of two palace buildings with marvelous gardens spreading between them. Both buildings are now museums devoted mainly to Austrian paintings.

The Ringstrasse leads through pleasant parks and plazas. One such plaza is the Karlsplatz. Dominating this public square is the massive dome of St. Charles Church. Built in the early 1700s, St. Charles is a splendid example of baroque architecture. Near the church stands the Historic Museum of the City of Vienna. Detailed models inside show the old city with the defensive walls (now the Ringstrasse) sweeping around its outskirts.

*St. Charles Church
on the Karlsplatz*

Berggasse (BAIRK-GAH-SUH)
Karlsplatz (KARLSS-PLAHTS)

The highlight of the Secession Building is a golden dome made of 3,000 cast-iron leaves.

Architects and artists are natural rebels. Many artists of the late 1800s criticized the buildings rising along the Ringstrasse. Yes, the structures were interesting to look at, but they imitated architectural styles of the past. Rebel architects desired something new. So they created the Secession Building near the Ringstrasse. With free-flowing curves and playful decorations, the building broke all architectural rules. Its highlight is a golden dome made of 3,000 cast-iron leaves. The Viennese call this stylized dome the "golden cabbage." The base of the building bears an inscription that sums up the rebellious architects' philosophy: "To Every Age Its Art, To Art Its Freedom."

A Shrine to Freud

Near the Ringstrasse is Number 19 Berggasse, once the apartment of Sigmund Freud. A graduate of the University of Vienna, Freud was a doctor who treated mental illnesses through a revolutionary method he called psychoanalysis. Freud lived and saw patients in this upstairs apartment from 1891 to 1938. The apartment, which contains many items of Freud's own furniture, now serves as a museum. His followers think of the place as a shrine.

BEYOND THE RING

A plaque with a painting of Schönbrunn Palace

One of the most splendid palaces in all the world is the Schönbrunn. Constructed in the 1700s, Schönbrunn Palace rose in a forest clearing that was a good distance from what was then the city limits. Today, the splendid palace is just a few subway stops from the Karlsplatz station. Guests enter through the vast gardens. The name Schönbrunn means "beautiful fountain." A pond and a bubbling fountain greet visitors. The palace grounds also contain a zoo. The zoo was established in 1752 and is considered to be the world's oldest.

Hapsburg Queen Maria Theresa looked upon Schönbrunn as a summer home for her family. Over the years, it became a head-quarters for Hapsburg power and pleasure. The dining room seated more than 100 guests. Dances held at the Schönbrunn were the most talked-about affairs in all Europe. The dances lasted only about four hours, the time it took for the candles to melt away. The ballroom was illuminated by 800 candles. Even though the Hapsburgs employed a small army of servants, the candles could not be changed fast enough to keep the parties going.

Left: The formal gardens at Schönbrunn Palace

Right: The Palm House on the Schönbrunn Palace grounds is a tropical greenhouse with a huge collection of exotic plants.

The Vienna Woods is a forested area just outside the old city. Be prepared to walk uphill as you explore this region. The Vienna Woods is the start of the Alps, Europe's tallest mountain system. Over the years, the woods and its small villages have been immortalized in song. Johann Strauss Jr. wrote "Tales of the Vienna Woods" about this pleasant region. Another musician inspired by the forest was Ludwig van Beethoven. Beethoven tramped over country roads in the Vienna Woods while composing music in his mind. His Sixth Symphony, the *Pastoral*, was written during his hikes. While listening to the beautiful *Pastoral* symphony one can almost smell the pine trees of the Vienna Woods.

Vienna glories in its past, but it is in every respect a modern city. The outlying areas hold the factories where cars and television sets are assembled. Modern Vienna is seen in the glass-and-steel buildings of the United Nations Center, an office complex where some 4,500 people work. The rural areas outside the city are also Vienna's playground. A huge park called the Donauinsel serves thousands of Viennese every weekend. The park is built along an island in the middle of the Danube River.

For ages, the waters of the Danube have flowed through Vienna. The river made Vienna a trading center and the capital of a vast empire. Monuments of empire still stand in the city's magnificent architecture. Its musical heritage is unmatched. Few other cities have preserved the past and faced the future as gracefully as has Vienna.

A Viennese girl wearing an Austrian folk costume

Above: The Vienna Woods viewed from the village of Kahlenberg

Right: The Upper Danube and the United Nations Center, a complex of office buildings

Donauinsel (DOE-NOW-INN-SELL)

FAMOUS LANDMARKS

Skyline showing the University of Vienna

Right: The Danube Canal
Below: St. Charles Church

The Danube Canal

Visitors might be a bit disappointed when they first see Vienna's portion of the Danube River. It is not "The Beautiful Blue Danube" glorified in the Strauss waltz. In fact, the stream that winds through old Vienna is the Danube Canal, and it is usually a brownish color. The main branch of the Danube River lies a few miles outside of town.

St. Stefan's Cathedral (Stephansdom)

In the heart of the inner city, "Old Steffl" is Vienna's most prominent landmark. It was first built more than 700 years ago. The church steeple can be seen from nearly every point in Vienna.

Hoher Markt

This is an ancient city square with several interesting features. The Anker Clock on the east end of the square comes to life at noon when mechanical figures representing historical men and women march out from behind doors. The square's St. Joseph Fountain portrays the marriage of Joseph and Mary. Also near the square are the Underground Roman Ruins, excavations showing Roman houses built some 2,000 years ago.

The University of Vienna

Founded in 1365, it is the world's oldest German-speaking university. The main courtyard holds statues of famous professors.

Burgtheater

Known to Viennese as "the Burg," it was built between 1872 and 1883. Its outside walls have carved figures representing dramatic human emotions—love, hate, humility, etc. A state-owned theater, it holds regular performances. The Burgtheater is one of many large and extravagant buildings built along the Ringstrasse in the years just after the old city walls were removed.

The New Town Hall

Only about 120 years old, this building is "new" by Vienna standards. The Town Hall is another example of glamorous architecture on the Ringstrasse.

Hofburg Palace

Once the home of the powerful Hapsburg family, the palace is a series of buildings constructed over a 700-year span. Within the palace grounds are a half dozen museums and the decorative stable where the world-famous Spanish Riding School gives demonstrations of horsemanship.

Right: The Anker Clock
Below: Hofburg Palace

Below: Schönbrunn Palace

Museum of Fine Arts

Another imposing building along the Ringstrasse, it houses one of the world's finest art collections. Egyptian sculpture as well as paintings from nearly every European art movement are displayed.

St. Charles Church (Karlskirche)

In the early 1700s, Vienna was struck by a deadly plague. Emperor Charles VI promised God he would build a church if the city were saved from the dreaded sickness. The plague subsided and, as promised, the emperor built this grand church.

Construction began in 1715. A park called the Karlsplatz spreads in front of the church and the Historic Museum of the City of Vienna is nearby.

Belvedere Palace

Two palace buildings separated by lovely gardens make this a Vienna treasure. Both buildings are now art museums.

The Prater

Vienna's popular park is a 3,200-acre (1,295-ha) people's playground. An amusement park with dazzling rides sits on its tip. The amusement park's 212-foot (65-m) Ferris wheel is a city landmark.

The Schönbrunn Palace

Built originally as a "summer home" for the Hapsburg family, the Schönbrunn is a "must see" highlight of Vienna. The palace has 1,200 rooms, but only about 45 are open to the pubic. In its heyday, the palace rang with music. The child genius Mozart gave a piano recital here when he was only five years old. When the boy Mozart finished his recital, he kissed the empress on the cheek and asked her to marry him.

The Vienna Woods

Praised in songs and poems, the Vienna Woods spread out from the city and contain country roads and quaint villages. This is wine-making country. Special wine taverns called Heuriger thrive here. One of the most interesting of the suburban villages is Grinzing, with its low-lying houses and twisting streets.

FAST FACTS

POPULATION   1,515,666

Vienna is Austria's capital as well as its largest city.

AREA   About 160 square miles
(415 sq km)

CLIMATE   Vienna enjoys a pleasant climate considering its central European location. Even in the middle of winter, the cold snaps do not last long. The average January temperature is 28 degrees Fahrenheit (-2° Celsius); the average July temperature is 72 degrees Fahrenheit (22° Celsius). Hot days in the summer are refreshed by the Wiener Lüfterl, an almost constant light breeze that blows in from the west.

INDUSTRIES   Vienna is Austria's leading industrial city. Factories in the city and suburbs produce automobiles and auto parts, radios and television sets, clothing, medicines, and chemical products. The manufacture of food products and musical instruments are also major industries. A thriving tourist industry provides many jobs in hotels and restaurants. Vienna is famous for its efficient public transportation, which includes streetcars, light rail systems, and buses.

CHRONOLOGY

15 B.C.
The Romans establish an outpost called Vindobona on the site of modern Vienna; previously, Celtic peoples had lived in the region for many centuries.

A.D. 400
The Roman Empire collapses.

800s
The Magyars, a people from today's nation of Hungary, take over the city, by now called Vienna.

1278
Rudolf of Hapsburg makes Vienna the capital of his empire; he is the first of many Hapsburg kings to rule from the city.

1365
The University of Vienna is founded.

1433
The tower of St. Stefan's Cathedral is completed.

1529
Turkish armies lay siege to Vienna, but are unable to capture the city.

1683
The Turks are defeated in a second attempt to seize Vienna.

1680–1740
Many baroque palaces and churches are constructed in the city.

1749
The magnificent Schönbrunn Palace is completed outside the city walls.

1766
The Prater, once a royal hunting ground, becomes a city park.

1791
Wolfgang Amadeus Mozart dies in Vienna; he is buried in an unmarked grave.

A little girl joins a line of men in Austrian folk costumes.

1848
Hapsburg prince Franz Josef becomes emperor and rules Austria for the next 68 years.

1857
The ancient city walls are dismantled and the Ringstrasse is built in their place.

1897
The giant Ferris wheel, now a city landmark, is built in Prater Park.

1914
Archduke Franz Ferdinand, a member of the Hapsburg family, is assassinated; the crime leads to World War I.

1918
World War I ends and the Hapsburg dynasty comes to a close.

1938
Adolf Hitler unites Austria with Germany.

1939
World War II begins in Europe.

1945
Vienna suffers devastating bombing raids; Soviet troops capture the city; a ten-year period of occupation begins.

1955
Occupation ends; Vienna and Austria are independent.

1969
Construction of the city subway system begins.

1979
The United Nations Center, a huge complex of buildings serving the United Nations' agencies, opens on the outskirts of Vienna.

1993
Austria joins the European Community (EC).

VIENNA

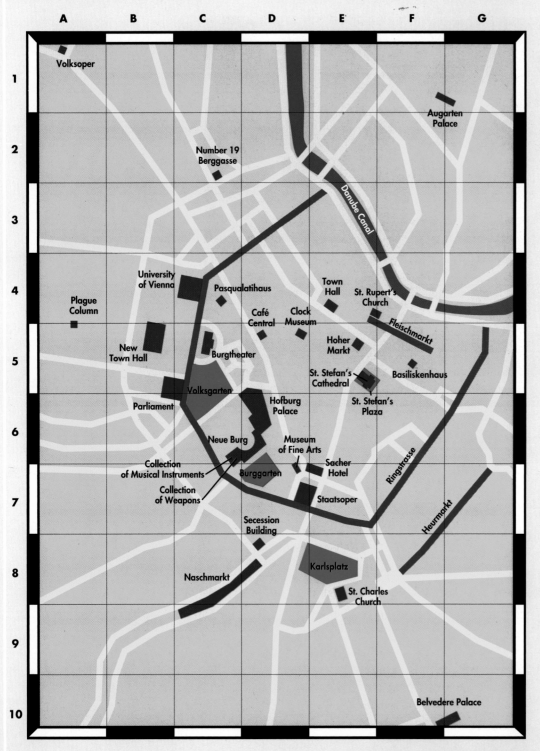

VIENNA AND SURROUNDINGS

St. Rupert's Church	E,F 4
St. Stefan's Plaza	E5
St. Stefan's Cathedral	E5
Staatsoper	D,E 7
Town Hall	E4
United Nations Center	K1
University of Vienna	C4
Vienna Stadium	J2
Vienna Woods	H1
Volksgarten	C 5,6
Volksoper	A1

GLOSSARY

babble: Confused languages; the term is taken from the city of Babel, as found in the Bible

Communion: In Christian practice, the sharing of holy bread and wine

coveted: Desired

fabulous: Extravagant, showing great riches

gaudy: A showy, rather tasteless display of clothes or goods

haggle: To argue over price

imperial: Referring to an empire or the time of empire

lavish: A display of riches or luxury

monarchy: Government headed by a king or queen

panorama: A splendid view over a wide area

prodigy: A young person who displays exceptional talents

solemn: Serious to the point of sadness

strategic: A key location from the point of view of trade

Wien: The German spelling for Vienna

Picture Identifications

Cover: Johann Strauss statue in City Park, Belvedere Palace, girls in Austrian dress
Title Page: Austria Fest costumes
Pages 4–5: Church on the Danube
Pages 8–9: Dawn at Belvederegarden
Pages 18–19: Vienna as it looked in 1780
Pages 30–31: Painting of a musical evening with Johann Strauss and others
Pages 42–43: Schönbrunn Palace

TO FIND OUT MORE

BOOKS

Austria: Facts and Figures. Vienna, Austria: Federal Press Service, 1994.

Fisher, Robert I. C. (ed.). *Fodor's Vienna and the Danube Valley*. New York: Fodor's Travel Publications, 1997.

Hughes, Helga, Bob Wolfe, and Diane Wolfe. *Cooking the Austrian Way*. Minneapolis: Lerner Publications Company, 1990.

James, Louis. *Passport's Illustrated Travel Guide to Vienna*. Lincolnwood, Ill.: Passport Books, 1997.

James, Louis and Johnn Richards. *Vienna Up Close: District by District, Street by Street*. Lincolnwood, Ill.: Passport Books, 1996.

Lerner Geography Department. *Austria in Pictures*. Visual Geography series. Minneapolis: Lerner Publications Company, 1991.

Orgell, Doris. *Devil in Vienna* (fiction). New York: Puffin Books, 1988.

Schrenk, Hans-Jörg. *Lipizzaner Horses*. Magnificent Horses of the World series. Milwaukee: Gareth Stevens Publishing, 1995.

Sheehan, Sean. *Austria*. Cultures of the World series. New York: Marshall Cavendish, 1993.

Venezia, Mike. *Ludwig van Beethoven*. Getting to Know the World's Greatest Composers series. Danbury, Conn.: Children's Press, 1996.

Venezia, Mike. *Wolfgang Amadeus Mozart*. Getting to Know the World's Greatest Composers series. Danbury, Conn.: Children's Press,

ONLINE SITES

American Football in Austria
http://www.opt.math.tu-graz.ac.at/ ~karisch/giants.d/austria.html
History, schedules, standings, and other information on the European and Austrian Team Conferences.

Austria
http://austria-info.at/
The official website of the National Tourist Office offers information about Austria, its provinces and cities, culture, events for young people, video, and links to related sites.

Schönbrunn
http://www.vie.at/camping/links.html
Visit the famous Schönbrunn Palace, take a virtual tour, learn about upcoming events, and sign the guestbook!

Vienna
http://www.anto.com/vienna.html
A sampling of the city's incredible art and architecture, including Schönbrunn Palace, Museum of Fine Arts, and the Vienna State Opera House.

Vienna and Viennese Art
http://www.geocities.com/Vienna/1605/ viestart.htm
History, art, classical music, museums, upcoming events, links.

Vienna City
http://www.atnet.co.at/Tourism/Vienna/
A wide offering of information, including popular attractions, restaurants, cultural events, concerts, and weather reports.

Vienna Scene
http://wtv.magwien.gv.at/welcome.htm
Museums, restaurants, events, special programs, photos, and plenty of attractions.

Welcome to Austria!
http://www.anto.com/
Austria A to Z, Alpine Adventures, a guide to the six Imperial Cities, and much more.

ABOUT THE AUTHOR

R. Conrad Stein was born and grew up in Chicago. After serving in the Marine Corps, he attended the University of Illinois, where he graduated with a degree in history. He later earned an advanced degree from the University of Guanajuato in Mexico. Mr. Stein is a full-time writer of books for young readers, with more than 80 titles published. He lives in Chicago with his wife and their daughter, Janna.

To research this book, Mr. Stein and his wife traveled to Vienna. They rode the streetcars, talked to the Viennese, went to the museums, attended the opera, and ate far too much in the city's wonderful restaurants. It was a thoroughly enjoyable visit.